To: Mrs Peggy

Let Wisdom speak!
Give Wisdom out.
Like candy

Pastor Herb

First Printing: 2019

ISBN 978-0-359-50356-8

Email: Herbert.addison@yahoo.com

Welcome to 31 days of wisdom and motivation! You have chosen to embark on a journey that will take you higher in the Lord! By the end of this study, you will develop a deeper relationship with God. It is suggested that each day you read 1 chapter of Proverbs and write what you learned in the note section of the book. There are motivational quotes designed to inspire you to live the life of a champion. Find a verse in Proverbs that speaks to you and meditate on it daily. Thanks for accepting the challenge may God Bless your journey!

Day 1

Proverbs 1:1-33

The reason for 31 days of Wisdom Unleashed is to help you develop a deeper understanding of God's Word. Day 1 begins explaining the purpose for Proverbs and expresses respect for God. The fear of the Lord will keep you from the pit. Wisdom is like a GPS it will help navigate you in your walk with God. Pray and ask God what he wants you to take away from this study. Find days to fast before the 31 days is up! God Bless!

Quote of the Day

66

Accept the people that God remove out of your life. It is necessary for growth. Pruning is apart of the process.

Wisdom Unleashed

NOTES

Day 2

Proverbs 2:1-22

Day 2 speaks of the life long journey of understanding God. The more we understand God the more we understand people. When you understand people you will know how to treat people. You will also understand the people you need to stay away from. Wisdom is a vision tool!

Quote of the Day

"

Do not stay in the cocoon longer than you need to.
The butterfly inside of you desires to fly. Do not make one
phase in your life permanent. Life will change just like
seasons.

Wisdom Unleashed

NOTES

Day 3

Proverbs 3:1-35

Hiding The Word of God in your heart is healthy. The Word teaches self-care. Often times, we are consumed with life and helping others and forget to study God's word. The word is a blueprint that explains how to avoid trouble, how to treat others, and how to conduct yourself. Proverbs 3 proves God wants his children to live a peaceful life. Peace begins with getting wisdom and understanding.

Quote of the Day

"

It is great to dream, but wake up and go to work. Make

your dream a reality. Do not get stuck in a dream for life.

It could turn into a nightmare.

Wisdom Unleashed

NOTES

Day 4

Proverbs 4:1-35

Day 4 reminds us of the importance of wisdom and understanding. We should get it at all cost! What has it cost you so far? If you cannot answer that question it is time to dig deep. If you can answer the question it is time to dig deeper. Wisdom protects you from those who desire to harm you. There are those who will try to kill your purpose, which is why you must get wisdom and understanding at all cost!

Quote of the Day

66

The bumpy road could be the fastest way to your destination. It does not matter how you get there as long as you reach your desired destination.

Wisdom Unleashed

NOTES

Day 5

Proverbs 5:1-23

Day 5 is dedicated to teaching on temptation. The temptation will come on every side but God is there as a teacher. This proverb explains how giving in to temptation can lead to the pit. Everyone is tempted and everyone can overcome because Jesus overcame temptation. There will always be a way of escape. Take heed to the teachings and examples of Jesus Christ.

Quote of the Day

"

Sometimes your blessing is just on the other side of the temptation. Make the adjustment and avoid temptation.

Wisdom Unleashed

NOTES

Day 6

Proverbs 6:1-35

Day 6 has several themes but begins explaining how unforgiveness can hold you captive. It encourages you to exhaust yourself trying to seek out forgiveness and also to be eager to forgive others. We stop our own progress when we do not forgive. You are a danger to yourself and halt your progress.

Quote of the Day

"

Celebrate your progress and acknowledge your progress. Break free from the bonds of unforgiveness and move forward.

Wisdom Unleashed

NOTES

Day 7

Proverbs 7:1-27

Day 7 expresses that God's Word is life. Following his commandments keeps us from the trap the enemy has set. The adulterous woman in this text represents the temptations of this world. The world has a lot to offer but all roads lead to death. The wisdom God gives leads to eternal life and gives instructions on how to avoid temptation.

Quote of the Day

66

A Miracle can be made from what you think is a mistake. If you fall into temptation repent, forgive yourself, and move into miracle mode.

Wisdom Unleashed

NOTES

Day 8

Proverbs 8:1-36

On day 8, wisdom is screaming at you! It desires for you to explore the possibilities. Material things cannot take the place of wisdom, however, it can help you acquire wealth. Do not confuse wealth for wisdom. Those who love wealth will receive death, but those who get wisdom will receive a life that leads to wealth.

Quote of the Day

66

You can predict the outcome of the fight when you put God first. Fight for wisdom because it will lead you to God for the answers you seek.

Wisdom Unleashed

NOTES

Day 9

Proverbs 9:1-18

On day 9, wisdom has prepared a meal and wants those who are worthy to partake in the feast. Everyone is not worthy to sit at the table. Those who are worthy increase in knowledge, but those whom it is not meant for will mock wisdom. Stop inviting people to the table who were not meant to be there.

Quote of the Day

"

Accountability is like the wheels on a vehicle. It is needed to get to your destination. Feast with those who are worthy of the meal. Everyone will not appreciate wisdom.

Wisdom Unleashed

NOTES

Day 10

Proverbs 10:1-32

Day 10 expresses that wealth acquired in the wrong manner will not last. Anything given or received with evil intentions does not prosper. Love creates an atmosphere for wisdom to grow and sin to be covered. Those who ignore wise teaching do not bear fruit and repeat a cycle of sin, which leads to death.

Quote of the Day

66

A dream that you had as a youth just may lead to wealth. A child begins life with pure thoughts; your childhood dream may be the key to your success.

Wisdom Unleashed

NOTES

Day 11

Proverbs 11:1-31

Day 11 is full of jewels! Proper balance is necessary for the wise. It is dangerous to indulge too much and not wise to work too little. Everything God allows you to obtain is not for everyone. The wise conceals precious jewels until it is time for them to be displayed. When all the jewels are gathered then the wise open a museum to display wisdom and understanding.

Quote of the Day

"

Museums only hold precious artifacts. The wise only hold on to information that educates. It is only displayed for those who appreciate beautiful artwork.

Wisdom Unleashed

NOTES

Day 12

Proverbs 12:1-28

Day 12 begins with expressing correction. Those who are able to accept correction are wise. Wise counsel should be consulted at all times. The actions of the wise match their words. Words alone are null and void. Action is the key. Laziness is a killer but hard work brings life to a deadly situation.

Quote of the Day

"

Laziness leads to poverty. In due season the hard worker will get noticed. The lazy worker gets noticed too and poverty becomes his love.

Wisdom Unleashed

NOTES

Day 13

Proverbs 13:1-25

Day 13 is filled with the theme of correction. Correction equals growth. The wise are always evolving. Evolution will happen, but some are lost in time. Time brings about change. A person must grow with time. Do not be upset because the wicked prosper and store up riches, because those riches will eventually end up in the hands of the righteous!

Quote of the Day

66

Your vision must be stronger than the distractions. Evaluate both

to see which one is winning. Glasses correct vision, but do you see

yourself through the eyes of God? Look to God for vision, you could be

your biggest distraction.

Wisdom Unleashed

NOTES

Day 14

Proverbs 14:1-35

Day 14 speaks of those who are liars and stir up trouble. God does not honor a false witness. Anger should not overtake the righteous. The wise take their time to think before reacting. The Word of God can determine the right way. Only the unwise will believe their way can save them. The person acting without God's guidance is headed for destruction.

Quote of the Day

66

Everyone has a destiny. Do not allow people to dictate how you get there. If you have to crawl, walk, or run it does not matter, just get there!

Wisdom Unleashed

NOTES

Day 15

Proverbs 15:1-33

Tone is everything. How you talk to a person can determine the outcome of a situation. True wisdom is thinking before you speak. Often times, our feelings make us react in a negative manner, but wisdom teaches patience. The patient person is honored in the eyes of God but those who allow rage to overtake them bring shame to their name.

Quote of the Day

66

Do not despise your struggle. The struggle creates passion and passion gives you the power to achieve.

Wisdom Unleashed

NOTES

Day 16

Proverbs 16:1-33

Day 16 speaks to pride. Pride is a silent killer. It is like a sniper at the top of a building knocking people off their high horse. Those who are walking with the prideful will suffer also. The fall is great and the person full of pride does not mind taking others with them. Remember Lucifer took some of the angels with him when he fell. Consult the Lord in all you do, for He is the master planner. We should be as children hanging on every word of our father God.

Quote of the Day

"

Get friends that push you to be great. Get friends that point you toward greatness. Get friends that pursue greater. Get friends that want the whole team to be the greatest.

Wisdom Unleashed

NOTES

Day 17

Proverbs 17:1-28

Wisdom cannot be purchased in a traditional manner. It is not sold at your local grocery store. There is a price for wisdom and everyone pays a different fee. The wise help the poor in love and do not seek a reward. Those who shame the poor mock God. Some people you meet will become more like family than your own. These individuals respect the God-given wisdom inside of you that can change their life. You obtain wisdom to share with those who will be students.

Quote of the Day

"

If grace had a face, what would it look like? If it were ugly would you still want it? Jesus on the cross is a picture of grace. The cross was ugly and beautiful. Do not be ugly. The same grace you desire be willing to extend to others.

Wisdom Unleashed

NOTES

Day 18

Proverbs 18:1-24

If one does not have wise friends eventually foolishness will overtake them. Jesus is the model for what friendships should be. He loved, taught, and even fed his disciples. However, friends should not be based upon what one can do for you. Riches corrupt even good people. Those who give to the poor in secret are rich beyond measure.

Quote of the Day

"

The true blessing is when you bless others. The true prayer is

when you pray for others. Who have you blessed or prayed for lately?

Wisdom Unleashed

NOTES

_____

_____

_____

_____

_____

_____

_____

_____

_____

_____

_____

_____

_____

_____

Day 19

Proverbs 19:1-29

Integrity should be favored rather than riches. The poor with integrity is rich but does not have many friends. The rich have many friends with a bad attitude and always receive things for free. On the other hand, the poor beg and are despised. People will rarely lend a helping hand to the needy. God will honor those who have compassion for the poor. Compassion is wisdom in action showing God's love.

Quote of the Day

66

Do not blame other people for your failures. When you accept responsibility a solution is around the corner.

Wisdom Unleashed

NOTES

Day 20

Proverbs 20:1-30

Harvest time equals work. Many want a reward but do not want to work. The time spent plotting on how to get over can be spent on how to make the work easier. The lazy end up in need, but those who work reap a harvest. Those who show love only to the rich have their reward, but those who love all people have a crown of life. Love forgives sin, but unforgiveness kills slowly. Anger can cause wars, but love can create a dialogue for peace.

Quote of the Day

66

Pain is a perfect recipe for gumbo. Your trials and tribulations can be used to make something good that will feed the next generation.

Wisdom Unleashed

NOTES

Day 21

Proverbs 21:1-31

Peace is better than conflict. The wise listen and respond with words of wisdom. A bribe reveals the true heart of a person. The Lord does not honor those who can be brought. It is better to have little money with integrity, rather than riches with no integrity. Pride holds a person captive, but the humble are free and obtain life. If you have compassion for others, God will have mercy on you. Everyone will need mercy and some point. It is only a matter of when. How have you treated others?

Quote of the Day

66

Work toward the future. Leave a legacy for the next generation. When your name is searched on Google in the future, what will your contribution to society be?

Wisdom Unleashed

NOTES

Day 22

Proverbs 22:1-29

A good name is better than riches. You cannot buy a good name it has to be earned. The company you keep reveals who you really are. Choose your friends wisely. An unwise friend leads everyone to shame, but the wise lift up his friends in need. Wealth received on the back of the poor leads to death and dishonor, but those who have compassion on the poor receive honor from God and build a good name.

Quote of the Day

66

If you have compassion for others, God will have compassion for you. There will be a time when everyone will want compassion. If you view your life, do you deserve compassion based on how you have treated others?

Wisdom Unleashed

NOTES

Day 23

Proverbs 23:1-35

Do not sit at the table with those who are jealous of you. They only seek information to bring you down. Dining with someone has a way of making a person comfortable even with the enemy. Do not desire the wealth of the wicked. Money that comes fast has wings. It flies south for the winter. There should not be a reward foolish behavior. Reveal it and the wise will change their ways. Everyone will not receive correction. Only invest in those who will receive it.

Quote of the Day

"

Prepare like you have already won the prize. Prepare like you already have the opportunity. Prepare like you are already on the next level. When you get there, repeat the process. In life, we are always making preparations for something.

Wisdom Unleashed

NOTES

Day 24

Proverbs 24:1-34

Wise counsel equals strength and power. Everyone should have counsel from a group of individuals that help them navigate through life. Do not covet the wicked that seem to prosper because their end is destruction. Wickedness should not be honored, but the goal is to show the lost that there is a better way. Strength is found in trials. Those who press through trials grow and receive a reward. The wise seek opportunities for growth, but the lazy is content with whatever is given to them.

Quote of the Day

66

Build on a foundation that can support your children. Build your children and they will become your foundation.

Wisdom Unleashed

NOTES

Day 25

Proverbs 25:1-28

The wicked corrupt good people. The saying is true one bad apple spoils the bunch. Remove the bad apple and the bunch will thrive. Too much of anything is not wise. Proper balance is the key to long life. A false claim will come back to haunt you. Use truth as a shield. It will protect you from a lying tongue. The truth is like a cold glass of water in the middle of the desert, it will save you from destruction.

Quote of the Day

"

When you feel that second wind kick in, that is an indication that you can win. Do not give up and wonder what could have been.

Wisdom Unleashed

NOTES

Day 26

Proverbs 26:1-28

Do not act a fool with those who do foolish things. Foolishness only leads to destruction. If the foolish is in any part of your life they will make it like a sideshow. It will be a circus. If you feed the animals they will keep coming to your house. Likewise, if you feed into foolishness it will become who you are and others will not respect you. Laziness does not receive honor. It only leads to begging and poverty. People will help a hard working person, but a lazy person becomes the talk of the town.

Quote of the Day

66

You cannot attend every event, take every engagement, or go to every party and be successful. Time is valuable choose wisely.

Wisdom Unleashed

NOTES

Day 27

Proverbs 27:1-27

Allow people to honor you. The humble are rewarded in due season, but the prideful have their reward. A friend in the dark is not a friend. Beware of those who will not acknowledge you as a friend in public. They gossip about you to others. A true friend sometimes will be there for you more than your family. They then become family. Trust should be gained and not be easily given. If the wise help the wise and they become stronger together, but two fools will stay fools.

Quote of the Day

66

History educates, emancipates, and can increase wealth. Educate your children on your family history. It may save them from the traps you fell into. Do not continue a negative family cycle.

Wisdom Unleashed

NOTES

Day 28

Proverbs 28:1-28

The upright stand strong and bold for what they believe in. A wise leader has compassion for the poor. The company of a polite poor person is to be favored over a rich person with a bad attitude. The inside of a man determines the measure of a man. The heart of a man tells his story, but love can rewrite the story. Confession cleans and sets one free from bondage. Holding on to sin locks you in a prison. Many are held captive because they refused to let things go. The wise choose freedom. Confess then move on and learn from your mistakes.

Quote of the Day

"

Too much of anything will push you over the edge. Proper balance will keep you from burnout. No balance equals no progress.

Wisdom Unleashed

NOTES

Day 29

Proverbs 29:1-27

The stubborn is not wise and will bring shame to the family. Ignoring the signs God send only leads to destruction. The poor should always be considered. A Kingdom is built on caring for those less fortunate. Individuals who only favor those who can do something for them shall not prosper. They will be known for their deeds. People are drawn to integrity but despise a con artist. There is no substitute for discipline. Correction saves the soul from death. Life can be found in the company of the wise, but everyone is not invited.

Quote of the Day

"

Mental health is just as important as physical health. Many people workout the body, but not the mind. You can lose your shape but if you have the right mind you can get your shape back. If you lose your mind you will not remember that you had a shape.

Wisdom Unleashed

NOTES

Day 30

Proverbs 30:1-33

Those who confess shall be saved. The wise understand who they are and know they are powerless without God. Understanding self leads to an amazing discovery, but loving self leads to all kinds of hidden treasures. As an ant stores up food in the summer, so should the wise save for a rainy day. Those who do not save become a borrower and end up in debt. A lion does not run from an opponent likewise do not run from trials. Be bold and fight!

Quote of the Day

66

When you treat people fair and equal people hear. When you do not treat people fair and equal people hear. How do you treat people? Ask yourself, because others have heard.

Wisdom Unleashed

NOTES

Day 31

Proverbs 31:1-31

The final day highlights a virtuous woman, but first, it warns about strange women, wine, and beer. This combination can cause a man to lose everything. A virtuous woman brings respect and wealth to her household. She completes her husband and makes the home strong. The household does not lack because she is like a ship carrying all kinds of goods. Any man can have a woman, but a virtuous woman comes from the Lord!

Quote of the Day

"

Be assured in whom God made you no matter what they say about you. They do not understand the struggle you endured to be who you are today. Who are they anyway?

Wisdom Unleashed

NOTES

Wisdom Unleashed

NOTES

Wisdom Unleashed

NOTES

Wisdom Unleashed

NOTES

Wisdom Unleashed

NOTES

_____
_____
_____
_____
_____
_____
_____
_____
_____
_____
_____
_____
_____
_____

Wisdom Unleashed

NOTES

Wisdom Unleashed

NOTES

Wisdom Unleashed

NOTES